ANIMAL CRACKERS

LIGHT VERSES IN AN ALPHABESTIARY

by
LEONARD R. N. ASHLEY

Jones Harvest
PUBLISHING

ISBN: 978-1-60388-025-1
1-60388-025-9

TO THE READER

A book like this is rather like a box of bonbons. Dip in and try a few, but do not try to digest the whole all at once. That might upset your stomach. Select a few and savor. Taste soft centers; never just push the bottoms in and put them back. Some are hard centers. Linger on them. And, of course, even if this is light verse it is poetry, meant to be read aloud and guided by the line arrangements. Do not read on public transport where if you laugh loudly or even smile broadly people think you must be crazy. Amusement is not crazy; laughter is good medicine.

Leonard R. N. Ashley

THE AARDVARK

Aafricaa
Is where aardvarks aare.
Not more colorful than
The orange - utan

ANIMALS' SOULS

Sir Edward Tylor took a look
At primitives, and in his book
He said such people, on the whole,
Think everything has got a soul.
So give respect to rocks and trees
And animals. And enemies.

ANTS

To the picnic come the ants,
Maybe with their uncles, too,
Moms and dads and cousins many,
Even if you don't want any.

THE APE

The ape, with antics and with bare behind,
Is woefully undignified, I find.
I'm deeply shocked, the way he lives.
That's true of all my relatives.

THE ASP

Cleopatra learned a lesson we all need.
Her last experience is something we should heed.
What to your bosom should you never clasp?
Don't asp.

ASSES

The asses bray.

It is their way.

He, haw, they are saying.

That's braying.

He haw, he haw.

He haw, she haw.

If you think I'm going to try the duck,

You're out of luck.

Some rhymes are really easy

But too sleazy.

You want some verses nearer to the
    bone,

Write your own.

THE BABOON

The baboon thinks attractive the part on
    which he sits.

        It's

        Not

        So hot.

This is a warning: Treat with caution

Every part and keep proportion.

If you want your stuff to strut

Examine if and and, and butt.

Not everything can you enhance

With your tight pair of capri pants.

THE BADGER

Live and let live's
A good motto, it's true.
If you don't badger badgers
Badgers won't badger you.

Leonard R. N. Ashley

BARNACLES

Barnacles stick to hulls and rocks.
Rockers stick with babes and jocks.

THE BASENJI

The basenji
Is ….
Expect no rhyme
This time.

Leonard R. N. Ashley

THE BASILISK

It may involve substantial risk
To gaze upon the basilisk.
So, even if they don't exist,
Resist.

THE BAT

The bat at night
Has flown (or flied).
That's why it's right
That he's red-eyed.

THE BEAR

When you see a bear,
Get out of there.
It's the safest thing to do.
This goes for all stock markets, too.

THE BEAVER

The beaver says working is being in Heaven.

He's there at his task most of 24/7.

But when the urge comes for a
bam-bam-bam-bam,

Well that's the time beavers will not give a
dam.

THE BED BUG

**The only good bed bug
Is a dead bug.**

THE BEE

Aerodynamic laws abound
To prove the bee can't leave the ground.
The busy bee is unaware
He has no business up there,
And so he soars aloft, not fearing
The principles of engineering.

THE BEETLE

Here's the beetle.
What he'll eat'll
Surprise.

BIRD SONG

Every bird you've ever heard cheep its little
    song,

Communicating, maybe mating,

Has been chatting all along.

Whether parroting or singing,

Always it's some message bringing,

Calling, flirting, warning, stalking….

Talk is cheap—but cheep is talking!

THE BISON

Did you know that is not a buffalo?
That is what we call a bison.
In Australian language placin'
A bison's what you wash your fice in.

THE BRANCHIOPODS

Some branchiopods sleep 15 years.

Like full professors may, my dears,

Dormant, not dead. They then take off

And spring to action playing golf.

Then comes the spectacle, oh my!

Emeriti, emeritae.

After the college has been teed off with these
elves,

They revive, they get active, they tee off
themselves.

THE BULL

The bull these days is apt to fuss.
His very name's synonymous
With something rude. He's often rated
Insensitive, and denigrated.
The reason's easy to detect:
He's not politically correct.
There's no excuse that can avail
A creature obviously male.

THE BULLDOG

Open your borders,
See what you receive.
If Britain's going to the dogs
It's not the British bulldogs, I believe.

THE BUTTERFLY
AND THE MOTH

We cast a loving eye
On the butterfly,
While the moth
Makes us wax wroth.
Our preference
Depends on terms of reference.
We can discern with hardly any fuss
(A) What is pretty (B) What is eating us.

THE CAIMAN

Some kinds of things we just don't want to see.
A caiman in a K-Mart is a big K-tastrophe.

CALVES

We get our clean and healthful milk
In cartons every day.
When calves seek out their nourishment
They have an udder way.

Leonard R. N. Ashley

THE CAMEL AND THE DROMEDARY

The camel and the dromedary
Make me very very wary.
I'm never sure—are you?—
About one lump or two.
In any case, your average camel
At heart's a most disgusting mammal.
The slightly different dromedary
Is somewhat nicer, but not very.

THE CASSOWARY

The cassowary cannot fly.
He has to walk, like you and I.
(Or, if grammatical you be,
It has to walk, like you and me.)
That is embarrassing, for a bird,
But he still does it, last I heard.
The cassowary is inscrutable.
That sometimes is as good as beautiful.

THE CAT

If you think you can teach a cat a trick,
You're sick.
Cats do what cats just want to do.
All cats are unconcerned with you.
A cat is a cat.
That's that.

CATALOGUE

A Siamese
Is hard to please.
A tabby
Can be crabby.
Burmese?
Oh, please!
A Manx?
No, thanks.
If you want a mouser around,
Go to the pound.
If you want a friend who'll think you're a star,
Try a bar.
Or an Irish setter.
Cats know better.

THE CATERPILLAR

How strange are the creatures
Of old Noah's ark!
Why don't we say a dogerpillar
On the tree bark?

Leonard R. N. Ashley

THE CENTIPEDE

The centipede is very wise.
He makes those legs all synchronize.

THE CHAMELEON

The chameleon changes color of its skin.

Maybe he's one of Michael Jackson's kin.

THE CHEETAH

The cheetah now we must confess
Fears nothing from the IRS.
And that is why the cheetah's smiling
He never heeds the April filing.
He suns, he hunts, he eats, more sunning,
And thus he keeps his business running
And all his pleasures always maxes
Without the fear of owing taxes.

CHICKEN

Fried chicken in Asian talk
Is cock of the wok.

Leonard R. N. Ashley

THE CHIMPANZEE

With food the chimp's a champ.

The chimp can chomp bananas.

With food the chimp's no chump.

But chimps are lacking manas.

Steal it,

Peel it,

Eat, and toss the peel,

Just like human litter bugs, some of you may feel.

THE CHUB

The chub, a fat and coarse-fleshed fish,
They say can make a tasty dish.
The sparkling river chubs' best place is.
The fishermen are chubby-chasers.

THE CLAM

The clam
Doesn't give a damn.
He eats, he mates, he takes a nap, he
Teaches us how to be happy.
So be a clam and sleep, mate, sup,
Or just shut up.

COATI MUNDI

Coati mundi is a creature
Whose name is its most noted feature.
Across our eyes it pulls the wool:
Its name sounds like a papal bull.

THE COBRA

See how the cobra starts to sway
When Indian fakirs start to play.
Since cobras don't have any ears
It's not the music that he hears
Makes him a dancer.
What's the answer?
More than the Rope Trick of that nation
That requires some explanation.
But Oedipus once made conclusive
The fact that some things now elusive
Should stay
That way.
OK?
So when you think about the cobra
It should only make you sobra.
And if you see a cobra in a basket,
Don't ask it.

THE COCKROACH

The cockroach saw the earth's first dawn.
He will be here when we are gone.
Forgetting this, we make a fuss
And say the world was made for us.

THE COW

The cow

Lives in the now.

Yesterday's over.

Today it's all clover.

Tomorrow, who knows?

And that's how it goes.

For the cow, that's essential.

We say, Existential.

Did you ever imagine philosophy's art

Could keep us all cowed by the thinking of
  Sartre?

THE CRANE

Why does that crane stand on one leg?
You ask with puzzled frown.
Because if he did not, of course,
The poor thing would fall down.

THE CROCODILE

Egyptians thought the crocodile
Was sacred, full of mystery.
If you approach the crocodile,
You may be history.
The crocodiles are not a friendly bunch.
One lunge, you're lunch.

THE CROW

If the crow looks old
It's no surprise.
He has crow's feet
Way under his eyes.

CRUSTACEANS

I do not have much patience
For crustaceans.
Shells hard or soft, I don't keep tabs
On crabs.
Lobsters taste vaguely of aluminum.
They live in shells without much room in 'em.

Leonard R. N. Ashley

THE DACHSHUND

The dachsund really likes to go
And get his dachs all in a row.

DEER

Some things should really not seem queer,
Like individual hopes, or fear.
The knights in Tennyson
Eating venison
Did not endear themselves to deer.

THE DIGGER WASP

Philanthus triangulum
Isn't mamalian.
It's called Digger Wasp,
But it isn't Australian.

Leonard R. N. Ashley

THE DINGO

**Would you call that wild dog dingo?
Bingo!**

THE DODO

The dodo, easy-going,
Today is really gone.
You must be more assertive
Or you won't continue on.
(Continue on's redundant
But rhymes are not abundant,
So please excuse this little stretch.
Don't quiz, don't quibble, and don't kvetch.)

Leonard R. N. Ashley*

DOGGIES

Yorkies are yappy,
And schnauzers are wild.
Why don't you people
Just go have a child?

A DOG'S LIFE

The dog that's out wants in.
The dog that's in wants out.
The dog lives life excitedly,
That's what he's all about.
But after he has run and played
Adventurousness tires.
Dogs like to curl up on the mats
In front of cozy fires.
No wonder "man's best friend" is what we call
The canine not so different from us all.

THE DONKEY

The donkey is so stubborn
That most folks can't abide one.
He is so damn intractable
That only Christ could ride one.
The donkey may seem dumb to us
But central in his story
Is one time very long ago
The donkey was in glory.

THE DOVE

**The dove
Is just a pigeon we love.**

Leonard R. N. Ashley

THE DUCK-BILLED PLATYPUS

The duck-billed platypus each day
Has twice it weight to put away
In worms.
Being a duck-billed platypus
Would not appeal to most of us.
Not on those terms.

DUCKS AND SWANS

Ugly duckling, lovely swan.
Do you believe that crap? Come on!
Just another tale of Momma's
That was proved an empty promise.
When you grow up and join the ducks
Reality, you find, just sucks.
You find the truth in later years
Of genes, silk purses and sows' ears.

THE EAGLE

The white-head eagle our national symbol has
   been called.

Is that because so many old Americans are
   bald?

THE EARLY WORM

The early worm winds up as bait.
So maybe you should get up late.

THE EEL

**The eel
Has no appeal.**

THE ELAN

The elan with *élan vital*
Is he-ing and she-ing and having a ball.

THE ELEPHANT

The elephant, for heaven's sakes,
Is one of Nature's big mistakes.
His life is just a hectic race
To find an elephant burial place,
And when at last the mammoth falls—
Umbrella stands and billiard balls.

THE EMU

Here is an emu, e-moting, e-mailing.
At the keyboard, never failing.
He says to you:
You have e-mu.

FAT CHANCE

Bergmann's Rule is simply that
Colder climates make you fat.
In colder climes the humans are hulkier,
And all the animals are bulkier.
So don't go on a diet to get skinnier.
Move to a place that's warmer thanVirginia.

THE FERRET

**The reputation of the ferret
As friendly pet he does not merit.**

THE FINCH

Life for the finch
Is a cinch.
Life can be easy for you,
   Too,
If you're content at the cage
   Stage.

THE FIREFLY

A firefly in a fight'd
Be de-lighted.

FISHY PROBLEMS

If the flounder flounders
Does a skate skate?
And does the Dover have a soul?
 Puzzles like these
 Are meant to tease
But are not useful, on the whole.
The ignorant can pose a question
That gives the wise man indigestion.

THE FLAMINGO

If a flamingo should light on your lawn,
If you simply say "Boo" the flamingo is gone.
The plastic flamingoes can never be scooted.
They stay put 'til the neighbors see that
    they're uprooted.

THE FLEA

If fleas have fleas
And other fleas
Pray upon parasites like these
It opens new philosophies.
Suggestions, please.

THE FLY

The fly walks on the ceiling upside down.
He has a very different view of town.
By doing this he gets a most selective
And quite unusual perspective.
    So we and the fly
    Do not see eye to eye.

FOWL PLAY

We take the eggs and, like as not,
Eventually into the pot
Go pullet, capon, rooster, hen.
Such is the fate of middlemen.

THE FOX

This fox is fixin'
With his vixen
To outwit the men in pink.
He may get by
Because he's sly
And hunters are not smart, I think.
Who would dress up to chase a fox?
Snob crocks!

THE FROG

The frog
On a log
In the bog.
The simplest poem possible.
But now simplicity's tossable
By poets who can't rhyme and won't
   communicate
And use free verse merely to be
   obscurely subjective.

THE FRUIT FLY

Fruit flies reproduce, as everyone knows,
They're heterosexual flies, I suppose.

THE GADFLY

The gadfly's a pest that is truly infernal.

You will find him with cattle or radical journal.

THE GAZELLE

We cannot all be graceful
As your average fleet gazelle.
That is really not disgraceful
And it may be just as well.
Nietsche's view on human features
He expressed in simple terms:
"You evolved from simple creatures
And you're still a lot like worms."
Though this judgment hardly flatters
It is good to keep in mind
For the thing that really matters
Is: to relatives be kind.
If you have a better fate or
Better looks or skin not fur
Just give thanks to our Creator
The Almighty Him, or Her.

THE GECKO

I think that even Art Deco
Is more attractive than a gecko.

THE GERBIL & FRIENDS

No gerbil
Does well on Verbal.
Nor does a calf
Score high on Math.
And that is why there's none of these
In leading universities.
They simply failed the SATs.

GHOST CRABS

Crabby old folks say: "Florida? Yes, sir!"
Adult ghost crabs New Jersey much prefer.
Each of these has its own requirement
For retirement.

THE GIANT SQUID

The giant squid
Likes to stay hid.
Should he come upon the scene
He can get mean.
If a squid you see,
Flee.

Leonard R. N. Ashley

THE GIBBON

For beauty the gibbon
Will win no blue ribbon.

THE GIRAFFE

This is a giraffe.
Don't laugh.
He stands upon his stilts
And tilts.
The effect is towering,
Overpowering.
So even if you cannot brook him
It's difficult to overlook him.
Without him there would be a gap in
The history of what can happen
If, dropping all your inhibitions,
You stretch yourself to meet conditions.

THE GNAT

**The gnat is gnot
Worth too much thot.
Yet it can lead to verbal games,
Inspire No-See-'Ems and such names.**

THE GNU

No gnus
Is good gnus.
Gnow you gknow
The gnews that's gnecessary.
Go.

THE GOAT

The goat will eat most things.
His dinner's unplanned.
He is not a gourmet.
He may be a gourmand.
But maybe gourmet is the rule at his tables:
He won't eat the cans, the goat just eats the
    labels.

THE GOLD BUG

The gold bug's not a bug.
He just feels funny
About money.

THE GOLDFISH

The goldfish. A reflective soul.
He watches us, outside his bowl,
And wonders what we're doing there,
Gulping so rhythmically for air.

GONE FISHING

There's a dogfish and a catfish
And a silverfish and goldfish
And an angel fish and devil fish
And damn near any kind you wish.
So many kinds, and I'm not blaming them
For what us people have been naming them.

THE GOOSE

Christmas time is here again,
Bringing joy to all good men.
This is not good news
For the goose.
(I'm sure you cannot have a perfect rhyme
Every time.)

THE GOPHER
AND FRIEND

The gopher is a tiny squirrel that lives out on
the prairie.
The gofer works in offices and may be John or
Mary.

THE GORILLA

The gorilla thumps his chest and bellows
Like lots of extreme wrestling fellows.

THE GREAT AUK

The Great Auk
Waulked the waulk
And tauked the tauk
But then it was regarded as *de trop*
And had to gop

THE GROUSE

**Wouldn't it be nice
If the plural of grouse was grice?**

Leonard R. N. Ashley

THE GUPPY

A guppy swims in tanks or else he
Is a guppie, lives in Chelsea.
Either one is likely dumb—
Aquarium, aquire-ium.

THE HAMSTER

The hamster's wheel, for exercise,
Much entertains the little guys.
So why have businessmen all found
Such tedium in the daily round?

THE HARPY

The harpy was of wings the proud possessor,
Unlike the Women's Studies full professor.

THE HAWK

The hawk is sharp-eyed and the hawk sees
    plenty.
The hawk has vision that is 60/20.
The less perceptive may not be much sappier.
If you don't see everything, you may be
    happier.

THE HEDGEHOG

The hedgehog is insectivore, a bug and fly
    man.
He just delights in bugs, like FBI man.

THE HERON

The heron
Has dignified bearin',
Long beak, long wings,
Long other things.

THE HIPPOPOTAMUS

A hyper hippo hardly plays
In waterholes Namibian.
More used to leisured, measured ways
Is this immense amphibian.
Now let us make the hippo's day
With hip and hip and hipporay.

THE HORSE

We like the horse,
Of course.
They have horse sense; they won't bet
On races in which humans get.

HOWLER MONKEYS

Here's a fate an African may fear:
Howler monkeys on the chandelier.

THE HUMAN ANIMAL

Of all the earth's animals, the only varmint
That wears a garment
Is us, I suppose.
The double-breasted seersucker is only one of
    those.

THE HYENA

The hyena
Sounds like the guy behind you at the sports
   arena.

THE IBIS

Egyptians thought the ibis was a god.
How odd!
It is amazing how the priests and laities
Imagine deities.

THE IGUANA

**What do you do if you're a male iguana
And the female iguana
Don't wanna?
An iguana's own looks are so really particular
They offer small chance for the
extracurricular.**

THE IRISH WOLFHOUND

The giant Irish wolfhound
Is the largest of the pets.
And what he wants that is around,
Well, that is what he gets.

THE JAGUAR

If you have to have a jaguar,
Buy a car.
The other kind's more dangerous
By far.

THE JAY

**The jay is brownish
And clownish.
And noisy.
Like mooks from Joisey.**

Leonard R. N. Ashley

THE JESUS BUG

Here is some news, dear son or daughter:
The Jesus bug can walk on water.

THE JELLYFISH

The jellyfish won't swim, he rides
Just back and forward with the tides.
He uses feelers for position.
He's rather like a politician.

JENNY

**The jenny's a female of donkey or bird.
Using one name for both seems completely
absurd.**

THE JERSEY COW

The Jersey's a cow
With one very big hooter.
His outside reminds me
Of Gateway Computer.

Leonard R. N. Ashley

THE KANGAROO

Some human parents take the tack
Of carting baby on the back.
But do you know who totes the runt
In little backpacks at the front?
The kangaroo,
That's who.

KATYDIDS

Shape and pattern of venation
Camouflage, prevent predation.
That's what katydids have done.
You could pick this trick, for one.
He who dresses as a victim
May discover bad luck's picked him.

THE KOMODO DRAGON

The dragon is a myth, fun style.
Often a myth is as good as a smile.
Komodo dragons need no wizards,
For they are real (and nasty) lizards.

THE LADY BUG

Lady bug, lady bug, fly away home,
You tiny, red, spotted millennium dome!
I wish you a kiss and affectionate hug
From a loving, considerate gentleman bug.

THE LAMB

Oh so innocent, the lamb!
He or she is not, by damn.
Every one, a he or her,
An invet'rate gamboler.

THE LARK

The lark each dewy dawn
At heaven's gate arises.
For getting up so early
I offer it no prizes.
I am a person of the night; the day's my
  adversary.
The only thing that gets me up is sex or
  mercenary.

THE LION

The lion is a kingly beast.
The lion thinks so, at the least.
It still is hard to sway, I guess,
His better half, the lioness.

Leonard R. N. Ashley

THE LLAMA

If you were to clone a llama,
It would have no dad or mama.
Not where you live or Alabama.
You could call it Dolly Llama.
But (get serious now) consider
The llama and the nearest bidder.
The two-L llama's furry and gymnastic.
The one-L lama's an ecclesiatic.
The difference is open to detection
On close inspection.

THE LOCUST

Some bugs eat any edible.
They're incredible.
The locust
Stays focust.

Leonard R. N. Ashley

THE LOUSE
AND THE NIT

The louse thinks the nit
Is it.

LOVE BIRDS

The love birds are charmingly other-directed.
But here is a fact you have never suspected:
Political feeling these last little whiles
Has demanded respect for alternate
    birdstyles.
And so you must look very close to determine
If it's Johnny and Mary or Henry and Herman.

LOVEBIRDS

Here are two lovebirds, extremely romantic.
They're caged with each other. That's better
    than frantic.
If you're stuck with someone, do not grow
    moroser.

            Get closer.

THE LYNX

A Canadian lynx
Must take care where it slinks.
A lynx on the links
Could put your golf off.

Leonard R. N. Ashley

THE MAGPIE

The magpie is felonious
And something of a fighter.
In these respects, and love of fuss,
He's like a sit com writer.

THE MALLARD

**The mallard
Does not inspire a ballard.**

THE MARMOT

There is nothing in a marmot
That would make you want to harm it.
Marmots conduct their sly affairs,
And you go your way, they go theirs.

MAY FLIES

**May flies are ephemeral
and will not last the summer.
Bummer.**

MICE

Are there mouses
In the houses
Or are there mice
In the hice?

THE MINK

How does a mink get another mink?
The same way chorus girls get mink,
I think.

THE MITE

The mite is tiny but he is a mad one.
The Bible claims a certain widow had one.
It must have been a deeply moving sight
To see her doing charity with all her mite.

THE MOCKINGBIRD

The mocking bird lights in the tree
And makes a few concessions:
He won't tell jokes or dance or rap
But does a few impressions.

MOHAIR

Here is a thing that I'd just love to know:
What kind of soft hair comes off of a mo?

THE MOLA MOLA

Just like the fatty body on the local beach
  behaves,
The mola mola (sunfish) basks while floating
  on the waves.

THE MOLE

The mole is blind
But moles don't mind.
In the life that they're pursuing,
There's not much worth the viewing.

MOLES

A mole's a spot, a spy, a pest.
It's hard to say which is the best.

THE MONGOOSE

**One mongoose we can leave at peace.
But two--mongooses or mongeese?**

THE MOOSE

This is a moose.
That is a mousse.
In Canada both are loose
Around the house.

MOSQUITOS

Mosquitos much resemble
A relative or two,
The kind that uninvited
Comes to put the bite on you.
Just zap 'em
Should this hapem.

MOTHS

**Moth debutantes perhaps hire halls
To hold moth balls.**

NATURE'S CONFUSION

Nature's seldom as you'd wish:
Silverfish is not a fish.
Earwigs have no ears or wigs.
See stag beetles on the their twigs,
Compare the stag.
What a drag!

THE NAUTILUS

In the Later Cambrian,
In Ordovician seas
Romped the huge invertebrates.
Nautilus is one of these.
He is in fact the sole descendant
Of that giant race, a remnant.
Likewise there were   earlier races
Of whom we simply took the places.

THE NEWT

A newt
Ain't cewt.

THE OCTOPUS

The octopus presents us with the Pentagon's
    weird charms.
Soft in the head
And full of dread,
He has a lot of arms.
He likes to brandish them at times,
Though that may not make sense.
He has a ravenous side to him.
His appetite's immense.
So let his tentacles reach out
But of his grip be chary.
And do not let some foreign guys
Turn him to calamari.

Leonard R. N. Ashley

THE OLD ENGLISH SHEEPDOG

An Old English Sheepdog's very hairy.
Very, very, very, very.
Significant Other thinks it's crime
If dog's not clipped in summertime.
The dog gets clipped. (S.O.'s a bully.)
I like dogs better fully woolly.
I don't know how the dog can take it
Furless but fearless, really naked,
When people sipping their martinis
At least wear thongs or sport bikinis.

THE ORANGUTAN

It's about time for that semi-man
The African orangutan.
Of praises he deserves so many.
It's just that I can't think of any.
The only thing that I can see:
He looks disturbingly like me.

THE OSTRICH

An ostrich hides his head 'cause he
Believes that you can never see
An ostrich if he can't see you.
        Un-true.
The moral of this tale is clear:
The weaknesses of you, my dear,
To all the rest of us appear,
        Not you.

THE OWL

The owl, 'tis said, is very wise.
The owl says Who. Mark that, you guys.
He won't say What. He won't say Where.
He won't say How. Just Who, and stare.
It ain't What, Where, When, How, I guess.
It's Who, you know, that spells success.

THE OYSTER

Few things are moister
Than an oyster.
He's about as wet
As wet can get.

Leonard R. N. Ashley

THE PANDA

The panda's loath to reproduce.
But being cuddly's no excuse
For one avoiding closer ties.
Another generation, guys!
You're born, you live, you ought to mate
And not too early. Or too late.

THE PANTHER

The panther is as black as ink.
See him slink.
Should he crouch to spring
Get the hell out of there for anywhere as fast
    as anything.

THE PARROT

The parrot gets some credit for repeating what
    he hears.
His unthinking repetition may persist for
    many years.
But you may not think that unreflecting
    parroting is bad
If you only will compare him with the average
    college grad.

THE PARTRIDGE

One cartridge,
Dead partridge.
That's why the partridges are hermits
And agitate *re* carry permits.
But gun laws won't save any thing or anyone.
The problem is the man behind the gun.

THE PEACOCK

The peacock likes to do his strut
With lots of feathers on his butt.
You may think this is most excessive,
But peahens think it quite impressive.
From this we learn that males will do
Whatever females want them to.

THE PELICAN

The Chinese says the pelican
Is un-Amelican.

Leonard R. N. Ashley

THE PENGUIN QUESTION

**Here is a question
To try on your friends:
If chickens have chicks
Do penguins have pens?**

THE PIG

Lazy pig, you should awaken
To the fact that you'll be bacon.
If you grow grossly obese
You will not be left in peace.

Leonard R. N. Ashley

THE PIGEON

You never see a baby pigeon.
They must start grown, not as a smidgen.

THE PIT BULL

The pit bull's named for his opponent
In old bull baiting, long since just antique.
Do not define yourself by opposition
Or stick with outworn labels from last week.

Leonard R. N. Ashley

A PLANKTONIC
ORGANISM

In the Lower Carboniferous or Mississippian time,
Was a small planktonic organism, but its name won't rhyme.
So I guess that's all we'll say of it . A passing nod will do.
But I like the sound of Carboniferous.

Say it twice. Don't you?

THE POLAR BEAR

Get a polaroid of a polar bear.

You'll see a bear is not so bare.

He must have all that fuzzy hair.

And that's because it's cold up there.

How'd you like to be sliding on the ice in wonderment

With nothing there to protect your fundament?

THE PORCUPINE

The porcupine is slow, sedate.
He thinks that keeping to himself is great.
His individuality
He guards with quills, for privacy.
He finds that if he takes that tack
No one will slap him on the back.
He'll never join, believe you me,
Kiwanis, Elks, or Rotary.

THE PORPOISE

The porpoise with his funny snout
Believes that life is bully.
He doesn't work, he just hangs out,
But does it porpoisefully.

THE POSSUM

Old possums are sly and when danger arrives
They pretend to be dead, thus protecting their
lives.
Take the possum's advice. This is how they
advise you:
Sit still at your desk and they may not
downsize you.
If you don't draw attention,
You may get to draw a pension.

PRE-HISTORIC CREATURES

The wooly mammoth

Had to vanoth.

The dinosaur—

No more.

The dinosaur got to be twenty feet tall

But his poor little brain remained so very
     small

He perished with the spacious ways

Of the Late Cretaceous days.

The moral: If your brain is weak

You won't be saved by your physique.

So—if you're dimwitted,

Destruction expect.

Think of Tyrannosaurus wrecked.

PTERODACTYLS

Pterodactyls once were found
Ptering around.
Now they're not.
Worth a thought.

THE PUG

I sometimes want to mug
A pug.
Especially those that –cheesh!—
Take dowagers for walks on leash.

THE PUMA

Take a puma for a pet
Endless trouble you will get.
The puma
Doesn't make a good ruma.

THE PUP

Here's a creature's had a pup.
Now she has to bring it up.
Many reproducers fail
To note what pleasure may entail.

Leonard R. N. Ashley

PURE-BRED PUPPY

Here's a yuppie
With a puppy.
The puppy has his papers,
The puppy is pure-bred.
As for the yuppie,
The less said....

THE QUETZAL

A quetzal basking in the sun.
He's very proud he's on the money.
OK, it's South American.
The quetzal does the best he can.

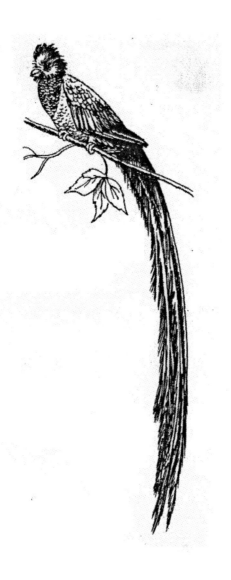

THE RABBIT

The rabbit has a habit
Of crinkling up his nose.
    I wonder if he,
    Sniffing at me,
Disapproves of people who
Make jokes about what rabbits do.

THE RACCOON

The old raccoon will very soon
Be checking out the garbage bin.
So put the lid on tight tonight
And do not let the raccoon in.
If, God forbid, it's insecure
It's garbage wall to wall for sure.
If you allow raccoons to get at it
You'll later find that they have et at it.

THE RATTLESNAKE

Before he joins battles
The rattlesnake rattles.
When strikes are a-borning
He likes to give warning.
The moral is—I think I have it right—
When you get rattled, you don't have to fight.

THE RAVEN AND THE HAWK

The raven

May be ravin'

But the hawk

Won't talk.

This reticence creates the reputation

Of hawks as sharper in the avian nation.

So, to impress, don't speak, stay mum instead.

'Nuff said.

REPTILES

**"All reptiles are cold blooded." That's a laugh!
Take one good look now at your office staff.**

Leonard R. N. Ashley

THE RHINOCEROS

The rhino. Example
Of what we learn quick:
If you're horny but ugly
Your skin must be thick.

THE ROBIN

Here's a robin doing good,
Singing for the robinhood.

THE ROOK

The rook is most gregarious,
Its habits multifarious.
Something of a crook
Is the rook,
Whom you may know
As a crow.

Leonard R. N. Ashley

THE ROOSTER AND FRIEND

The rooster crows, but the crow's best booster
Would never claim the crow can rooster.

THE ROUNDWORM
AND FRIEND

**The roundworm and the big horn sheep
Prove onomastic skill can sleep.**

THE SALMON

The salmon is our lesson for today:
When old age comes, it's upstream all the way.

THE SEAGULL

**The seagull's a seabird you don't have to dread
Unless, like hard math, it is over your head.**

Leonard R. N. Ashley

THE SEAL

The seal can balance a ball on his nose.
I really admire little talents like those.
God knows what the seal will come balancing
  nex'.
For myself, it is hard just to balance my
  checks.

THE SHARK

No wonder the shark is the meanest in town.
He has to keep swimming or else he will
    drown.
Some people in business themselves have
    such pressure
And have to keep working and keep saying
    "yes,sir!"
So, when next you meet someone that you
    wouldn't sup with
Please consider the life that they have to put
    up with.

SHEEP

Soon ev'ry creature on the earth
Will sport a cell'yar phone.
Even the sheep will have those things,
Not shepherds all alone.
At the moment sheep just eat
      And bleat.
Soon we shall hear the sheep
      Beep.

THE SHREW

A little piglet is a suckling.
A baby duck is called a duckling.
A newborn shrew is called a shrew.
Who knew?

THE SIAMESE

The Siamese kitty
Is pretty.
But you can't please
A Siamese.
They are mischievous as elves,
Siamese! Stuck on themselves!
They're standoffish, their heads whittled.
They make owners feel belittled.
They do not live with you, domesticated.
You live with them, and you are underrated.

SILVERFISH

The silverfish is not a fish.
All language should make sense. You wish.

SIZE MATTERS

Every gnat
That's begat
Reminds us that the mastodon
Is gone.

THE SKUNK

If you have sense
You'll leave skunks unmolested.
The skunks have scents
You could regret you've tested.

THE SLOAT

**There never was a sloat
Of note.
But sloats do
Not read *Who's Who*.**

SLUGS

Right in your garden there is a bout:
Here are some slugs slugging it out.

Leonard R. N. Ashley

A SMART FISH

Here is a fish
That ain't no fool.
Here is a fish
That stays in school.

THE SNAILS

California imported some edible snails.
They brought in some females, they brought
   in some males.
Then they started to breed with a great
   impropriety.
Immigration can cause certain woes for
   society.

THE SNAKE

Consider the snake?
Give me a break!
If you insist
One I must list,
Here's one bad guy that you are liable
To meet in life if not The Bible.
Black mambas are no kind of dances.
And with them you should not take chances.
This fellow grows to 15 feet.
He stands upon his tail. (That's neat.)
This way he strikes at 12 feet tall.
He might do well at basketball.

THE SPANIEL

Feeding my spaniel, how I wish
He'd keep his ears out of the dish.
His mistress, or so it appears,
Can't keep her dish out of my ears.

THE SPARROW

The sparrow
Has a view that is narrow
Of urban living.
It may be crumby
But fills his tummy,
So he's forgiving.

THE SPHINX AND THE GRIFFIN

The sphinx and the griffin were carpentered
Of other creatures, so we've heard.
A bit of something else and partly lion,
They were not welcomed much in ancient
    Zion.
No sir.
They weren't kosher.

THE SPIDER

Here is a spider, line name Jeb,
Who's chatting on the worldwide web.
He thinks he's talking to a fly
But it's another spider guy.

THE SQUIRREL

The squirrel is a kind of rat
A fuzzy tail disguises.
We do not think the squirrel's a brute.
As cute, he wins some prizes.
I want to tell you in this ditty:
If you're a rat, at least be pretty.
A cute tail
Can much avail.

Leonard R. N. Ashley

STORKS

If "storks bring babies" is only for the dorks,
Just tell me, then, who brings the baby storks?

Leonard R. N. Ashley

THE STURGEON

The sturgeon gives us roe. I wish he
Would not make caviar so fishy.
But still we eat it, feeling pensive
About the fact that it's expensive.
The way they make us think it's nice is
Simply to jack up the prices.

THE TADPOLE

The tadpole has a little tail
He loses when maturing.
Quite like an older husband after marriage,
Sometimes during.

TAKING TERNS

The tern's a bird that makes a lovely lover.
You know that one good tern deserves
   another.

THE TAPIR

You wouldn't want a tapir
For a napir.
Suppose he
Gets nosey.

THE THRUSH

Hush! The thrush
Sings on the bush.
Sight rhyme
This time.
This is a trick some poets are employing.
You may find it most annoying.

THE TICK

The tick
Can make you sick.
So please,
No Lyme disease.
Get away from a tick
Quick.

Leonard R. N. Ashley

THE TIGER AND THE LEOPARD

The tiger cannot change his stripes
But never gripes.
The leopard cannot change his spots
But worries lots.

TOADS

Toads by far
Have the worst PR.
Toadies need roadies
Or Swifty Lazars.

THE TORTOISE

Wherever the tortoise might roam,
He's home.

THE TOUCAN

At the zoo, and for a price,
One can see a toucan in a thrice.

THE TROUT

Look at that human wading out,
Hoping to outwit a trout.

Leonard R. N. Ashley

THE TUNA

The tuna is a fish that man's
Able to fit in little cans,
But man has not devised machinery
To cut out crowding in sardinery.

THE TURKEY

The turkey may not realize his living
Is any reason for thanksgiving.

Leonard R. N. Ashley

THE TURTLE

The turtle slowly carries on
Whether he's single or he marries.
He has no debt, no mortgage harries.
His house is what the turtle carries.

THE UNICORN

The unicorn prevented mergin'.
You'd only catch one with a virgin.
And that is why, with that proclivity,
No unicorn is in captivity.

VEGETARIANS

Most vegans won't eat meat but do eat fish.
Could they be logical? You wish!
I won't eat plaice.
Or anything with a face.

THE VIRUS

The virus reproduces in a cell
Or in a home computer very well.
Don't expect me to be admire-y
Of viri.

THE VOLE

Some tee-tiny rodents we like to call voles.
Of the beasts of the field they are most like the
proles.

THE VULTURE

The vulture's business-like if skirting.
His hovering is disconcerting.
Just one oops
And he swoops.

THE WALLABY

**This either is a wallaby
Or a wallaby wannabe.**

Leonard R. N. Ashley

THE WALRUS

The walrus (or whale horse) is nothing
   infernal.
He looks most of all like an old British
   colonel,
The close resemblance due, in my belief.
To obesity, the moustache and the teeth.

THE WAPITI

The wapiti
Is upiti.

Leonard R. N. Ashley

THE WASP

This is a wasp.
A WASP's another thing.
On either kind of creature,
Can you find the sting?

THE WEEVILS

If you're offered choices mean
In midst of life's upheavals
Take advice from Augustine:
Choose the lesser of two weevils.

THE WEREWOLF

The werewolf is only an old wife's tale.
But if you should meet one, then take to the
   trail.
A werewolf can be very scary,
And fooling with one could be hairy.
Run like hell.
A werewolf doesn't wear well.

THE WESTERN EQUITORIAL APE

The western equitorial ape
Is awfully hairy, but our shape.
He weighs up to a quarter ton.
He can't, however, fire a gun,
So man remains the anthropoid
It's most essential to avoid.

THE WHALE

The whale, folks say, can sing. Like opera divas
He's vocal and he's built like wide receivas.

THE WHIPPOORWILL

The whippoorwill's a funny bird known by his
    call, you see,
Like the heavy-breathing person who phones
    you at half past three.

THE WILDEBEESTE

In the minority at least
Is the Oscar Wildebeeste.
His rations
Are green carnations.
Conventional attitudes are news to it.
It's here, it's queer, so you— get used to it.

THE WOLF

A wolf is a predator , canine or male.
If you run into one it is time to turn tail.
The sailors are worst, or so I have hoid.
The wolf is ship's clothing's the one to avoid.

Leonard R. N. Ashley

THE WOMBAT

Imagine that you see a wombat
And the creature's locked in combat
With another little wombat.
Imagine hordes of these rapscallions
Wombattling in their wombattalions.

THE WORM

**When you die if they don't decide you should burn
It's the worm's turn.**

THE YAK

Sometimes you get a pet
You haven't tried yet
And, once within your walls,
It palls.
If somebody borrowed my yak,
I wouldn't ask for it back.

THE YETI

This Betty,
She's a yeti.
She is with her sister Mary.
Mary's also rather scary.

THE ZEBRA

"Why," the zebras ask with irritation,
"Do we come late and with no illustration?"
Anything else would be heretical
Because the book is alphabetical.
Here is a picture. Don't get in a stew.
I'll end with the book with a zebu.

THE ZEBU

The zebu
Are few
But, if you please,
I'll put one here to end the Zs.

Leonard R. N. Ashley

L'ENVOI

Now I thank you for attention
To my comical invention.
No ponderous poetry I rehearse.
It may be bad but could be verse.
It's not Sir Thomas Mallory's
    But—no calories.

ABOUT THE AUTHOR

Leonard R. N. Ashley (PhD, Princeton), LHD (Columbia Theological, hon.) is Professor *Emeritus* of Brooklyn College of The City University of New York and most of his several dozen published works are academic, covering literature (literary biography, literary criticism, literary history) and linguistics (onomastics, geolinguistics) and popular culture and folklore, the occult, and military history, plus textbooks. However, he did publish when younger in 50 or 60 poetry magazines that "died to make verse free". His latest books suggest his wide range. They are *Last Days* (dealing with *The Messiah*, *The Rapture*, *The Apocalypse*, and *The Last Judgment*), *Mexico: The Smart Traveler's Guide to All the Names* (for tourists who have no Spanish), and *Nordic Folk Lore and Tradition* (written with Ola J. Holten of Sweden). Some of his work has been translated into German, Dutch, and Portuguese but these little verse wordplays probably can't be.

Leonard R. N. Ashley